George Müller

Other titles in Heroes of the Cross series

To be published shortly:

GEORGE MÜLLER

Roger Steer

Marshall Pickering

Marshall Morgan & Scott
Pickering & Inglis
34-42 Cleveland Street, London W1P 5FB
Copyright © 1984 by Roger Steer

First published by Marshall Morgan & Scott 1984
Reissued in 1989

ISBN: 0 551 01138 6

Typeset by Preface Ltd, Salisbury, Wilts.
Printed in Great Britain by Courier International Ltd,
Tiptree, Essex

Contents

1: The prisoner

'George,' said his father, 'turn out your pockets!'

The boy laid out the contents on a table, and watched as his father examined them. Desperately he hoped there would be no further questions. Herr Müller looked hard at his son and then spoke again.

'Take off your shoes.'

George removed his right shoe.

'Let me see it, son.'

George handed it to his father.

'And now the other, please.'

George reluctantly presented his left shoe for inspection. It contained the exact sum of money which his father had discovered was missing from his desk.

After George Müller's birth, just three weeks before Nelson defeated the French Admiral Villeneuve at the Battle of Trafalgar in 1805, his mother and father had hoped he would grow up to make a career in the church. It was not that they wanted him to serve God, for they rarely thought much about that sort of thing, but that he might live comfortably as clergymen did in Prussia in those days. Before long, however, it looked as though they would be disappointed. Every child is naughty sometimes: but this one turned out to be worse than most.

When George was four his father had become a tax collector for the Prussian Government. The family had moved from Kroppenstaedt to Heimersleben and before his tenth birthday George had begun to steal Government money from his father. The punishment for taking and hiding the money in his shoe was, as usual, severe but it made little difference. George was a thoughtful child and spent a lot of time working out how he might do the same thing again more cleverly so as not to be detected.

One Saturday evening when he was fourteen, George's mother suddenly became ill. George did not know this or that his mother was longing to speak to him and hold his hand for what she knew would be the last time. He had gone to play cards with his friends from Halberstadt school. The games continued until two on the Sunday morning and then the group moved on to a tavern. Later they emerged and toured the streets, half drunk, before George returned home. His father was waiting for him looking pale and drawn.

'Your mother is dead,' he said.

George was shocked and stunned. But not long after the funeral, his behaviour grew worse rather than better. The day before he was confirmed, he tricked a priest by handing over only a twelfth of the fee which his father had given him.

After his first communion in Halberstadt cathedral at Easter 1820, George made up his mind to turn over a new leaf and spend more time at his studies. But his resolution was soon broken and for the next twenty months he spent more of his time drinking in taverns, playing the piano and guitar, reading novels, and making resolutions to improve than actually getting on with his school work.

Towards the end of 1821 he broke away from his school and travelled to Brunswick in search of freedom and adventure. He booked into a hotel just outside the town and spent a week living in luxury. When asked to pay he had no money and was forced to leave some of his clothes instead.

Next he moved to Wolfenbuttel, a charming little town with a medieval castle nestling in the hills of

Lower Saxony. He took a room at an inn and began another week of comfortable living. After some days, the landlord became suspicious and presented Müller with a bill. Unable to pay, he went quickly to his room and began to pack. There was a knock at the door: it was a policeman.

'George Müller?'

'Yes.'

'You are under arrest!'

He was led away and questioned for three hours. There was little he could say in his defence: he was penniless, and hopelessly in debt. With no indication as to when he could expect a trial, two soldiers marched him away – to prison.

His cell was small and dark, and lit only by a narrow window covered with strong iron bars. Thick wooden walls divided it from the cells on either side. The heavy door was bolted and locked: there was little chance of escape. That evening, he received some meat with his bread, but he hated the smell of it and left it untouched. This must have upset the chef, for there were no more special favours. On the second day he was treated to the same menu as his fellow-prisoners: for lunch, bread and water; for dinner, vegetables but no meat. Beginning to feel distinctly underfed, he ate a little.

Müller was locked in his cell day and night. He was given no work and no exercise. To help pass the time, he asked the warder for a Bible, but his request was refused. On the third day he ate all his food, and after the fourth, would always have been glad of more.

After some days, he discovered that there was another prisoner in the cell next to him. He shouted through the wall and learned that his neighbour had been a thief. Maybe to reduce the noise level of the conversation that followed, the governor allowed the two prisoners to share Müller's cell and they spent their time describing their adventures. Warming to his task, Müller began to invent stories which impressed his friend immensely. After about ten days, the two cell-mates disagreed and from that time they refused to speak to each other.

On January 12th 1822, the silence was interrupted by the sound of the unbolting of the cell door. It was the keeper of the prison.

'You are wanted at the police office. Follow me, please.'

The police commissioner looked up from his desk.

'You are a lucky young man, George Müller. Your father has sent the money which is needed to pay for your travelling expenses, to pay your debt at the inn and hotel, and for your stay in prison. You are therefore free to leave at once.'

Herr Müller celebrated his reunion with his son by beating him very hard. George tried hard to win back his father's favour. He made progress with his studies and began to teach younger pupils. He succeeded at last in regaining his father's affection.

When he was seventeen, Müller transferred to a college at Nordhausen, one of the oldest towns in Prussia. Once again, he began to disgrace himself. For one thing, he seemed quite unable to make ends meet and got himself seriously into debt. Once, after receiving an allowance from his father, he purposely showed the money to some of his friends. Then, he carefully damaged the locks of his trunk and guitar case. A few minutes later he ran into the director's room with his coat off, and announced, breathlessly, that his money had been stolen.

10

Everyone was wonderfully sympathetic. Some of his friends kindly clubbed together and managed to give him as much money as he had lost, while those who had lent him money agreed to extend their loans. However, the director – older and wiser – was suspicious and was unable to trust Müller again.

When he was nineteen, Müller entered the old and famous university of Halle in Easter 1825. He made another resolution to change his life for the better. This time he really meant it, but yet again, his resolution came to nothing. The freedom of university life offered all sorts of temptations and George Müller found it almost impossible to manage his money. He had to pawn his watch and some clothes; he began to borrow heavily from his friends. He felt utterly miserable: worn out by his many unsuccessful attempts to mend his ways.

It was in one of Halle's taverns (where he once drunk ten pints of beer in a single afternoon), that Müller thought he recognised a young man from his old school at Halberstadt. They had not been close friends, for Beta had been quiet and serious, but it occurred to Müller that if he struck up a close friendship now, it might help him to lead a steadier life. He picked his way across the crowded *Bierkeller* and shook Beta warmly by the hand.

'Beta! How are you you? How nice to see you after so long!'

'George Müller! I hardly recognised you.'

One of Müller's great delights was travel. He suggested to his friends that they should make a trip to Switzerland.

'But,' they said with much sense, 'we have no money, and no passports.'

'Leave it to me,' replied Müller. He persuaded his friends to forge letters from their parents which entitled them to passports. He arranged that the group pawned all they could to obtain the money they needed for the trip.

The party, which included Beta, travelled via Frankfurt and Zurich to the heart of Switzerland. They never forgot their first sight of Lake Lucerne, through a rising mist, and hemmed in by steep limestone mountains. There was no railway then, but they climbed the Rigi and the view took Müller's breath away. He looked at the great mountains which thrust themselves into the lake: Burgenstock, Seelisburg and away to the south-west Pilatus, all so irregular but magnificent. 'Now,' he thought, 'I have lived!'

They arrived back in Halle at the end of September, 1825. None of Müller's friends found out that the man they had trusted with their money had cunningly arranged things so that he himself paid far less towards the cost of the expedition than any other member of the party.

If George Müller was going to change, it would need a miracle.

2: The turning point

The friendship between George and Beta grew deeper. One Saturday afternoon, about the middle of November 1825, they were out for a stroll in Halle. As they talked, Beta grew serious.

'For some weeks I have been going to a meeting on Saturday evenings at the home of a Christian.'

He paused, wondering how George would react.

'And what happens at this meeting?'

'They read the Bible, they sing, they pray, and someone usually preaches a sermon.'

'I should like to go with you, this evening.'

'I'm not sure that you will enjoy it.'

George had made up his mind. 'I'd very much like to go.'

'Then I will call for you this evening.'

George hoped that going to the meeting might help him keep his resolutions to behave better. But he felt sure that Herr Wagner, at whose home the meeting was held, would not welcome him. He apologised for coming, but Herr Wagner smiled.

'Come as often as you like; house and heart are open to you!'

He ushered George and Beta in to join the others and they sat down. George was fascinated by the way the meeting was conducted and by what was said in the sermon.

As they walked home, George said to Beta:

'Nothing we saw and enjoyed in Switzerland can compare with this evening'.

It was the turning point of his life; and that night he lay peaceful and happy in his bed.

The next day and on several days during the following week, Müller returned to Herr Wagner's house to talk and to study the Bible with him. The verse that especially struck him was one of the best loved in the Bible: 'For God so loved the world that he gave his only Son, that whoever believes in him shall not perish but have eternal life' (John 3:16).

Realising how much Jesus must have loved him, Müller resolved to love him in return. He asked God to forgive his sins, as he put it, 'through the blood of Jesus'. Müller had become a Christian.

Six or seven weeks later, Müller decided that he wanted to become a missionary. The more he prayed about it, the more it seemed the right thing to do. But he was disappointed to find that his father did not like the idea.

Two years were left before he was due to complete his course at Halle, but he did not allow his studies to keep him from telling others about his new-found faith. He handed out gospel tracts, tried to persuade people he met to trust in Christ, and wrote to all his friends in the same way. He began to preach in the villages and towns surrounding Halle and became part-time chaplain in a local prison.

On Saturdays he continued to enjoy the meetings at Herr Wagner's house, and a group of students began to meet in his rooms on Sunday evenings.

In Easter, 1828, he passed his final exams and received his degree, despite all his other activities.

Müller now decided that he wanted to tell Jews about Jesus; and the London Society for Promoting Christianity among Jews (today the Church Mission to the Jews) agreed to accept him as a student.

In February, 1829, he left Berlin for London. On the way he visited his father at the home in Heimersleben where he had spent his childhood. At Rotterdam the river was still ice-bound, and no steamers dared venture out. After a month the weather turned warmer, and Müller boarded a ship bound for England. On March 19th, 1829, he arrived in London.

3: All for God

In 1829, London was more modern than any city Müller had seen in Europe. Large parts of its central area had recently been rebuilt by John Nash and Pall Mall was lit by gas lamps.

Müller found somewhere to live, not in the beautiful West End, but in Hackney. He worked very hard, for about twelve hours a day, mainly studying the Hebrew language which he would need for his work amongst the Jews, and trying to become fluent in English.

In May he fell ill. He had been far from well when he left Germany, and the long hours of study took their toll in London. He felt sure he was dying and could not stop thinking about the way he had lived as a teenager. Then he realised that all his sins had been forgiven through the blood of Jesus shed for him on the cross at Calvary. This restored his peace of mind and he decided that what he wanted more than anything else was to die and go to live with Jesus.

But this was not to be. After a fortnight, his docter told Müller he was getting better and suggested that a change of air was needed. Thus it was that he made his first visit to south Devon, the country where he would later spend over two years, although this stay lasted for less than three months.

It was at Teignmouth, in that summer of 1829, that Müller struck up a friendship with a young Scotsman which would last thirty-six years. The two men had a great deal in common. They were both nearly twenty-four; both had become Christians while university students; both were intrigued by the study of Hebrew; and both had – in words

16

which Müller used of Craik – a 'warmth of heart towards the Lord'.

Through Henry Craik, Müller came into contact with a group of young men who loved the Bible and were determined to take what it said seriously. They believed that when Jesus said, 'Sell your possessions and give to the poor' (Luke 12:33), and 'Do not store up for yourselves treasures on earth' (Matthew 6:19), he meant it. They practised what they preached.

One of the young men was a successful dentist in Exeter. He and his wife gave up first a tenth, then a quarter of their income and distributed it to poor people in their neighbourhood. Then they decided to abandon any idea of saving money or putting some aside for their children: they cut down their expenses by living more simply and gave away all the rest of their money.

George Müller described what happened to him that summer as 'like a second conversion'. Many years later he wrote a letter to a friend in which he said that during that stay in Devon he gave himself fully to the Lord. 'Honour, pleasure, money, my physical powers, my mental powers, all was laid down at the feet of Jesus, and I became a great lover of the Word of God. I found my all in God.'

Müller returned to London in September. Before the end of the year he began to wonder whether he should continue to be connected with the London Society for Promoting Christianity amongst the Jews. He now felt that he would like to serve God amongst Gentiles as well as Jews. But before making up his mind, he decided to spend a few months praying about it.

Early in the new year (1830) he made what he planned would be another short visit to Devon. As

17

things turned out, however, he never returned to London as a student. Faced with a growing number of invitations to preach in Exmouth and the surrounding areas, he decided to end his link with the Society he had come to England to serve. The break was a friendly one, and Müller never regretted the decision he had taken.

After three weeks in Exmouth, Müller left for Teignmouth intending to spend ten days with friends he had made during the previous summer. Henry Craik asked him to preach at the Baptist chapel across the river at Shaldon and, on hearing Müller preach, a young lady became a Christian. At further meetings more people were converted.

Then members of the congregation at Ebenezer Chapel, Teignmouth, invited Müller to become their Minister. He decided to accept, but made it clear that he would only stay with them as long as he was sure that it was God's will. His starting salary was £55 a year, but this sum was quickly increased as numbers joining the church began to grow.

4: Working together

Throughout the summer of 1830, Müller never refused a chance to visit Exeter. It was not only the beauty of the journey along the coast road from Teignmouth to Starcross and then by the Exe estuary to the county town that he enjoyed. The main attraction lay at the end of the journey: Müller had fallen in love.

The young lady who had caught his eye – Mary Groves – was the sister of the dentist who had given nearly the whole of his large income to the poor and who had since gone as a missionary to Persia. Mary shared her brother's love of the Bible and his determination to take what it said seriously. She was a good pianist and artist and spoke three languages, including – Müller discovered – Hebrew.

In August, Mary received a letter from George asking her to be his wife and four days later he arrived in person anxious to know the answer.

'Yes,' was the reply and the couple knelt down asking God to bless the marriage that was to take place. October 7th was the date of the wedding conducted in St David's Church, Exeter. After the reception they drove in a stage-coach to Teignmouth and, with no thought of a honeymoon, began to serve God together the following day.

Soon after returning to Teignmouth, the newly-married couple decided that it was wrong for George to receive a fixed salary. They abandoned the system by which people paid for their seats in the chapel, the better seats being more expensive. Instead a box was placed in the chapel with a notice which said that anyone who wanted to help support Mr and Mrs Müller could put their offerings inside.

It was at this time, too, that Müller made another important decision. From then onwards he would never ask anyone, not even one of his Christian friends in Ebenezer Chapel, to help him financially. The way he put it was that there would be 'no more going to man, instead of going to the Lord'. George and Mary began to take even the smallest things to God in prayer; and in this way discovered that he was a loving God.

During nearly two and a half years at Teignmouth they were always well provided for, although on some occasions the provisions arrived only just in time. And George's yearly income was always greater than the fixed salary he had abandoned. The congregation at the little chapel George had taken over grew from eighteen to fifty-one.

In April, 1832, Müller reminded his congregation that when he had become their pastor, he had warned them that he would stay only as long as he felt it was God's will to do so. He believed that God might have other work for him to do.

In May, he announced that he and Henry Craik had accepted an invitation to become the pastors of Gideon Chapel in Bristol. Both men were still only twenty-six; but the things they had learned at Teignmouth would stand them in good stead for the far greater work that lay ahead.

5: Cholera in Bristol

There was a time when Bristol had been second only to London in importance as a port but by the early nineteenth century Liverpool, with its miles of deep and windy estuary, had overtaken its rival. However, Isambard Kingdom Brunel did much to maintain the city's prestige by building the railway line to Bristol and the steam-ships *Great Western* and *Great Britain* in the city's docks.

The Müllers and Henry Craik found a large flat which they shared. As well as their work at Gideon Chapel, they were offered a large and modern building in the heart of Bristol – Bethesda Chapel in Great George Street. A friend provided the first year's rent.

On one Sunday, Müller would preach in the morning and Craik in the evening; the following Sunday it would be the other way round. From the earliest days they attracted much interest, with Bethesda becoming crowded particularly on Sunday evenings. Part of the attraction for some was the strangeness of their accents – Craik preaching in broad Scots and Müller with not only a strong German accent but also a tendency to get some of his words wrong. Müller was himself amused to hear of one lady who came to hear him preach just because she had been told of some words which he could not pronounce properly. But, as he recorded in his diary, 'scarcely had she entered the chapel, when she was led to see herself a sinner'.

In July, 1832, cholera broke out in Bristol and by August the outbreak had become a major crisis. Müller and Craik showed great courage throughout and carried on their work undaunted, visiting many cholera victims day and night.

In the middle of the epidemic, Mary Müller was due to have a baby. As her labour began, she became very ill, though not with cholera. Müller spent a whole night in prayer; next day Mary gave birth to a daughter. Despite everything, mother and child did well. They called the little girl Lydia.

A week later, Müller and Craik were called out to visit a woman who was seriously ill with cholera. It was one of the worst cases they had seen. The poor woman was crying out so loudly they could hardly say anything to her. Müller felt as if he himself was beginning to suffer from the disease.

When the two men arrived home they prayed that they would be kept from contracting cholera. Their prayer was answered; but the woman they had visited died. By October, the epidemic had passed its peak and life in Bristol began to return to normal.

Two years later, the Müllers' second child, Elijah, was born and the family decided to move into a house of their own. They chose a solid end of terrace house in Paul Street, High Kingsdown, with four storeys. It had a small garden which Müller often used for praying and thinking.

In June, 1835, when Elijah was fifteen months old he became ill with pneumonia. In their alarm, George and Mary prayed fervently. There were times in the early years of his Christian life when Müller felt God gave him a special gift of faith which enabled him to pray quite specifically for someone's healing. On this occasion, however, he did not feel able to do this. On the 25th he wrote in his diary:

'The Lord's holy will be done concerning the dear little one'.

The next day, Elijah died. Several years later, Müller wrote:

'When the Lord took from me a beloved infant, my soul was at peace; I could only weep tears of joy when I did weep. And why? Because my soul laid hold in faith on that word in the Bible: "Of such is the Kingdom of Heaven". Believing this, my soul rejoiced, instead of mourning, that my beloved infant was far happier with the Lord, than with me'.

Lydia was the only child of their own that George and Mary were able to love and care for, and to watch grow into adulthood. But, as we shall see, there were hundreds of other children, without parents themselves, who Mr and Mrs Müller were soon to welcome into one of the most remarkable families in England.

6: Pitied by one

At about the time that George Müller and Henry Craik moved to Bristol, Charles Dickens was becoming famous as a writer. One of his books was *Oliver Twist*, published in 1837, but serialised before then. He wrote it, as he always did, to entertain but also to make people think hard about the desperate plight of England's orphans.

He described the baby Oliver as 'despised by all, and pitied by none'. The most orphans could hope for from the Government was to be sent to a parish 'workhouse'. A new law in 1834 had deliberately set out to make the workhouses unpleasant places so as to discourage healthy but lazy adults from taking advantage of them. Conditions in the workhouses quickly became disgraceful and the poor children who were sent there because their parents had died, and had no relatives to look after them, had the worst possible start in life.

Leah and Harriet Culliford were not characters in one of Charles Dickens' novels. They were real children who lived in Bristol in 1835: Leah was five and Harriet nine. Their parents were poor and had become ill with tuberculosis. At that time there was nothing that doctors could do to treat this dreadful disease. One day, Leah and Harriet – who loved their parents dearly – were told:

'Your mummy and daddy are dead.'

The news was shattering and the future was grim. None of their relations could afford to have the two girls live with them for long. They would try desperately hard to avoid sending the children to a workhouse but there might be nothing else they could do.

In 1835 there were not many orphanages in England. Dr Barnardo founded his first home in 1866, and Mr Spurgeon followed in 1867; the National Children's Home, Fegan's Homes and the Church of England's Children's Society followed later.

The present writer knows of only a dozen orphanages which date back to the 1830s. They were all small and there was none in Bristol. Leah and Harriet would have had no chance of being admitted to eleven out of the twelve homes.

The first thing that would have kept them out of nearly all the homes was lack of money. Only one of the homes, in Southwark, had been set up to care for poor children and charged no fees. The other homes raised their funds and decided which children to receive by means of a horrid procedure known as the 'voting system'. In order to gain a place for an orphan child in one of these homes, a relative or guardian needed to secure a sufficient number of votes from 'subscribers' who would back their votes with subscriptions of money to support the child. Children were admitted in order of votes cast. Alternatively a wealthy friend or relative could buy annual or life subscriptions. George Müller once heard of a poor woman, a widow, who spent day after day attempting to obtain votes for one of her fatherless children and was so worn out that one day she came home exhausted from her efforts, sat down and died.

The second thing that would have kept the two Culliford girls out of all the homes except the one in Southwark was snobbery. The details these homes put out made it clear that they were intended for the children of 'middle class parents' or 'parents who had seen better days, and moved in a superior station in life'.

Some of the homes refused to receive children who were diseased or deformed and others those who couldn't read.

George Müller heard about Leah and Harriet Culliford through his Sunday School work. They were just two of many thousands of children made orphans at this time usually because their parents died of tuberculosis. Müller was one of the first men in England not only to want to do something positive to ease the problem, but to do it in a way which would help the poorest children rather than those who had wealthy or influential friends. When he first arrived in Bristol he had been upset by the common sight of children begging in the streets; and when they knocked on his own door he longed to do something practical to help.

While a student at Halle, Müller had lived for two months in one of the great orphan houses built by the German Professor A. H. Franke in the late seventeenth century. He had not forgotten his time there, and late in 1835 he began to think seriously about doing something similar.

He spent many hours praying about the possibility of opening an orphanage. He asked himself whether the whole idea did not stem from a desire to win glory for himself. He called on Henry Craik so that his friend could probe his motives. Craik duly probed; but found nothing to which he could object.

'My advice is that you should go ahead,' said Craik, 'and I shall give you every support and encouragement.'

Müller's concern for the plight of orphans in nineteenth century England began rather more than a year before Dickens made the situation widely known in *Oliver Twist*.

Quite apart from his genuine anxiety to help poor children, there was another important reason why he toyed with the idea of founding an orphanage. He wanted to show people that there really was a Living God; or, as he put it, that there was 'reality in the things of God'.

Many times as he visited the members of his two congregations in Bristol he found that people needed to have their faith strengthened. Once he visited a man who was in the habit of working at his trade for nearly sixteen hours every day. His health was suffering and his Christian faith meant little to him.

'If you worked shorter hours,' suggested Müller, 'do you not think that your health would improve, and you would have more time to read your Bible and pray? I believe you would be far happier.'

His friend looked doubtful.

'But if I work less, I do not earn enough to look after my family. Even now, while I work such long hours, I have hardly enough. Wages are so low, that I must work hard in order to obtain what I need.'

'This is not trust in God,' thought Müller. 'This is not belief in the words of Christ, "Seek first his kingdom and his righteousness, and all these things will be given to you as well." ' He replied:

'My dear brother, it is not your work which supports your family, but the Lord; and He who fed you and your family when you could not work at all when you were ill, would surely provide for you and yours, if, for the sake of spiritual refreshment, you worked fewer hours a day.'

As he waited for the reply, Müller looked at his friend's expression. It was clear that he agreed the advice was good; but there was still doubt. He was not prepared to trust completely in God.

'How can I be sure?' he replied. 'How can I be sure that if I followed your advice, things would be alright?'

Müller was not annoyed. He was sad. He thought, 'How I long that there was something to which I could point this man. Something that would act as a visible proof that our Father is still the same faithful God as he always was; as willing as ever to prove Himself the Living God, in our day as in the past, to all who put their trust in Him.'

Müller met businessmen who claimed to be Christians but who were not honest in all that they did. They suffered from guilty consciences, but argued that they could not afford to behave in any other way. Afraid to trust God fully, they preferred to rely on their own devices. To these people, too, Müller longed to demonstrate that God had not changed: that He would honour those who acted with integrity.

At Teignmouth, and now in Bristol, Müller had proved that trust in God worked. He received no salary, but God provided for him and his family. He longed that others should enjoy the same experience. He certainly did not want people to be lazy: he worked long hours himself. Rather he wanted people to know that they could safely take God at His word and rely upon His promises.

So Müller decided that he needed to set about something, simply through trusting in God, which, as he put it, could be 'seen, even by the natural eye'. He had decided to embark on one of the most exciting adventures in the history of the Christian church.

He was not a wealthy man, and he had no private

income. But he reasoned like this:

'If I, simply by prayer and faith, could obtain, *without asking any individual*, the funds to establish and run an Orphan-House: there would be something which God could use to strengthen the faith of Christians, and persuade those who are not Christians that God really does exist and that He answers prayer.'

7: A home for Leah and Harriet

On the evening of 9th December, 1835, Müller addressed a meeting about his plans for the orphanage. At his side was John Corser, who had been a clergyman, and who now intended to assist Müller in his work. Müller said:

'The home will only be established if God provides the means and suitable people to run it. But I am becoming more and more convinced that this project is His will. Now, if so, he can influence His people in any part of the world – for I do not look to Bristol, nor even to England, but to the living God, whose is the gold and silver – to entrust me and brother Corser, whom the Lord has made willing to help me in this work, with the means.

'No charge will be made for admission to the home and no child will be barred from entering it on grounds of class or religious belief.

'All who wish to be engaged as teachers, matrons, and assistants will have to be both true believers in the Lord Jesus Christ and appropriately qualified for the work they wish to do. Only children who have lost both their parents will be received. Any orphans whose relatives are able and willing to look after them will not be received: the home will be for children who are genuinely in need.

'Girls will be trained for various forms of service, and boys for a trade; the older children will be given useful work to do, and thus help to maintain themselves. The children will receive a plain education.

'The special aim of the institution will be to seek, with God's blessing, to bring them to the knowledge of Jesus Christ, by instructing them in the scriptures.'

When Müller had finished speaking there was

purposely no collection; however, he was given fifty pence. A woman offered to help in the work and Müller left the meeting feeling happy and quite sure that he would one day be able to open his children's home.

Next day he received a letter from a husband and wife who had decided they would like to work in the home if Müller thought them well enough qualified. What is more they had decided to give all their furniture to the home and work without any salary, simply trusting God to supply their needs. Other people offered to work in the same way.

Lots of gifts arrived which were just what would be needed in the home – furniture, cutlery, clothing and materials. One evening there was a ring at the Müller's door-bell. They opened the door not to a visitor but to – a kitchen fire-guard and dish, left, it seemed, by someone with strong views about giving to God secretly.

Money began to be sent as well. One lady, who earned much less than fifty pence a week from needlework, gave one hundred pounds. It was part of some money she had been left by a relative who had died: she had given some to her mother and used the rest to pay some family debts. Müller visited her and tried to persuade her to think again about her generous gift. She replied:

'The Lord Jesus has given His last drop of blood for me, and should I not give all the money I have? Rather than the Orphan-house should not be established, I will give all the money I have.'

Müller left the house not only with the £100 but with a further £5 which she insisted he took for needy members of his two churches.

Müller was now talking about opening a small

home in April 1836. It would be for girls between seven and twelve. He spent a whole evening praying that people would apply to send children to the new home, and the next day he received the first application.

He heard about a house, No. 6 Wilson Street, not far from Gideon Chapel, which was to be let at a low rent. Müller prayed about it and went to inspect the property. He found that it was a large terraced house, three storeys high and solidly built. He decided to rent it for at least a year and began to furnish it for thirty children.

April 11, 1836, was a day which Müller never forgot, for it was then that the first children arrived. One of them was named Harriet – Harriet Culliford. She looked anxiously at Mr Müller. He was a young man, still only thirty, who didn't look as if he would stand much nonsense. But he had a kind and calm expression on his face as he introduced each of the children to the smiling matron and governess. Neither Müller nor his helpers could give these little girls their mums and dads, but they were determined to do all they could to make good the loss.

Müller thought about the task that lay ahead. Every day, three times a day, for seven days every week there would be thirty hungry children to feed, plus the staff. Thirty pairs of feet would wear out thirty pairs of shoes; clothes would grow too worn or too small and need to be replaced. Müller knew that if ever the children were hungry or badly clothed, people would say there was no God, or that He did not answer prayer. But he was not alarmed; instead he would repeat to his family and helpers the words of Jesus in Matthew 6:31 and 33: 'Do not worry, saying, "What shall we eat?" or "What shall we drink?" or "What shall we wear?" But seek first

His Kingdom and His righteousness, and all these things will be given to you as well.'

At the end of September, a Bristol doctor offered to treat the children and supply medicine without charge. Müller gladly accepted. Gifts continued to arrive including four and a half gallons of beer, but we do not know whether the children were allowed to indulge.

Not long after opening his first home, Müller realised that there was a need for a home which provided for children under the age of seven. In November (1836) the first children began to arrive at No. 1 Wilson Street which Müller had managed to acquire for infant boys and girls. The building had a piece of land attached to it which the children used as a playground. Some of the eldest girls from No. 6 helped in the running of No. 1. Leah Culliford was one of the first children at the infant home.

Preparations were soon under way for the first Christmas in Wilson Street. If it was anything like later Christmases at Müller's homes, for which we have records, pretty decorations were made and put up; a large Christmas tree was loaded with toys and presents; special carols were learnt; and little shops were opened with sweets provided by the large Bristol manufacturers. We do know that on that first Christmas in 1836, a number of ducks and turkeys – and a hundredweight of treacle – arrived at Wilson Street.

By June, 1837, George Müller had received one thousand pounds for his orphan work. All this money and other gifts had been given to him without anyone ever being asked. Müller wanted lots of people to see God's hand at work, be encouraged to trust Him completely and know that He answers prayer.

8: A change of air

What was Müller to do with the infant boys when they reached the age of seven? The need for a further home was clear, and in October 1837 Müller was offered another of the houses in Wilson Street – No. 3. He decided to use it to provide a home for forty boys aged seven and above.

By the end of the year, eighty one children and nine full time staff sat down to meals in the three homes. In addition, Müller was now running a number of schools in which three hundred and fifty children were taught; and he had three hundred and twenty children in his Sunday School.

Perhaps because of all this work he had taken on, Müller's health broke down. He was suffering from what he at first described as a feeling of weakness in his head, and was unable to work. In November, 1837, he left Bristol to stay for a while in Bath. But there he found even conversation too much effort and returned to Bristol after some days afraid that he was going mad. He went to see his doctor.

'Your nerves are certainly disordered,' his doctor told him, 'and you have a problem in your liver. But you have no reason to fear that you are going insane'.

Müller was reassured. But the new year did not get off to a start which would be good for his nerves. On new year's day, burglars broke into his house. Fortunately they could not get into much of the building because of a second strong door and they took nothing but some meat. They then made their way to the school room at Gideon Chapel, broke open several boxes but took nothing. The burglars seem to have had an odd sense of humour: next day some bones, less the meat, were found – some in the boxes at the Gideon school room and one in a tree in Müller's garden!

It was too much for poor Müller, in his state of health. He visited his doctor again.

'What you need is a change of air. Can't you leave Bristol for a while?'

Müller was not keen. There was so much work to be done at Wilson Street, in the schools and at Bethesda and Gideon Chapels. But then a letter arrived from a lady who lived fifty miles from Bristol and could not possibly have known what the doctor had told him. She enclosed £15 which she said was 'for the express purpose of change of air'.

'This,' thought Müller, 'is an indication of God's will in the matter'.

He travelled with Mary and Lydia to stay with some friends in Trowbridge and settled down to read the *Life of George Whitefield*. The book cheered him up, although once or twice he felt ashamed that he had spent so much time on his knees reading Whitefield's Life rather than his Bible! However his physical health did not improve and after some weeks he moved on to stay with friends in Oxford.

There in the ancient university town he decided to try his hand at horse riding. He managed to hire a well-behaved and docile horse.

'This will suit my troubled nerves,' he thought.

For some days things went well and the students grew used to the sight of Müller riding his placid horse. But then – alas – the horse himself was taken ill! Müller returned to reading his Bible and prayer until he was told that the horse was well enough to resume his duties.

Back to the stables he went and climbed again on to the saddle. To his great dismay he discovered that the animal which had once been so well-mannered had now become stubborn, self-willed and almost impossible to control. Desperately he tried to control the beast but it was no good: George Müller would have to return to shanks's pony.

From Oxford he travelled to Leamington Spa where Mary rejoined him. Together the couple took walks in the Warwickshire countryside and George's head began to feel better than it had for several months, although he was still far from well.

In those days, people put great faith in the value of a change of air and Müller decided that a trip home to Germany might do him good. His doctor approved of the idea and in April Müller boarded a ship bound for his homeland. The sea was rough and he suffered badly from sea-sickness.

He stayed with his father and brother and spent some time telling them of his faith in Jesus. Perhaps his native air did help, for he began to feel better than he had for ages.

In May, he returned to England and on the 8th attended the prayer meeting at Gideon Chapel. It was the first time he had spoken at any meeting at Gideon or Bethesda since the previous November. But that evening the congregation at Gideon were delighted to hear again the familiar Prussian voice. He read Psalm 103.

'Praise the Lord, O my soul; all my inmost being, praise his holy name. Praise the Lord, O my soul, and forget not all his benefits. He forgives all my sins and heals all my diseases . . .'

George was nearly thirty-three. The man whom the army had rejected, claimed many years later that he felt fitter in his seventies than he had in his thirties.

9: Jehovah Jireh

From the day that George Müller opened his first children's home in Wilson Street in April 1836 to the end of June 1838, he never had to worry about money. There were always more funds available than he needed. But as the summer of 1838 drew towards its close, things became more difficult. This was the beginning of an anxious period which lasted until the end of 1846.

It was not that the children were ever hungry. Rather it was that God supplied the needs of the homes day by day, even sometimes hourly. One evening during these trying years, Müller wrote in his diary:

'These dear little ones know nothing about it, because their tables are as well supplied as when there were hundreds of pounds in the bank, and they lack nothing.'

Another day he wrote:

'The orphans have never lacked anything. Had I had thousands of pounds in hand, they would have fared no better than they have; for they have always had good nourishing food, the necessary articles of clothing and so on.'

The period from September 1838 to the end of 1846, although difficult, was not one of continuous trial: instead there tended to be a pattern of a few months of anxiety followed by a period when there was more than enough money available.

Why did God allow this time of 'trial'? We cannot be sure. Müller thought he could understand it best when he thought of the Old Testament story of Abraham and Isaac. God tested Abraham's faith by telling him to offer his only son as a sacrifice: when

37

He saw that Abraham was ready to obey Him even in this way, he provided a ram to be sacrificed instead. So, almost at the start of Müller's long years of children's work, God was testing his willingness to trust Him and obey Him.

Mr Rose, who is in charge of the Müller Homes for Children today, thinks that these were the years when Müller's character was moulded. God was preparing him for his life's work, strengthening his faith, teaching him that prayer works. 'He learned so much and really knew His God.'

Whatever the reason for these difficult years, they certainly make the story of this period an exciting one.

Just once during these years, it seemed to Müller that God was not answering his prayers.

The incident occurred in September 1838. On a Tuesday morning, Müller reviewed the situation at Wilson Street. His assistant at that time – who Müller used to refer to as 'Brother T' – had 25 shillings (£1–25) in hand and he himself had three shillings (15p). (Through most of the last century, a farm worker earned 50p a week and beer was one old penny a pint.) There were about one hundred people, including staff, to feed and care for in the three homes.

'With this money,' Müller said to Brother T, 'we can buy the meat and bread which we require; a little tea for No 6, and milk for all three homes. There is nothing more we need for today and we will then have bread in hand for two days. But how will God provide for the rest of the week? Our funds are exhausted. Let us meet for prayer.'

The staff met, as they did every morning, to pray

38

together. They then got on with the duties of the day, but no more money came in. In all three homes the children sat down to a good lunch and after lunch Müller returned to his home in Paul Street and began to pray again. Still no money arrived. How would he face the children tomorrow and announce that there was no breakfast? He described himself as 'tried in spirit'. Some years later he remembered this day and wrote:

'For the first time, the Lord seemed not to regard our prayer.'

In the middle of the afternoon, Müller's door bell rang. A woman introduced herself to him.

'I arrived in Bristol four or five days ago from London and am staying next door to the boys' home in Wilson Street. Before I left, my daughter let me have some money for your work which I have come to give you.'

She handed Müller an envelope.

'I am most grateful to you, and I shall of course write to your daughter to express my thanks.'

They talked for a while, and when the lady had left Müller opened the envelope. It contained over £3 – enough, at that time, to provide comfortably for all the following day's needs in the three homes.

Müller was not an excitable or emotional man, but that night he recorded in his diary that the moment he was alone, following the lady's visit, he had 'burst out into loud praises and thanks'. He took the fact that the money had been so near the houses for several days without being given as proof that, in his words, 'it was from the beginning in the heart of God to help us; but, because he delights in the prayers of His children, He had allowed us to pray so long; also to try our faith, and to make the answer so much the sweeter'.

One Wednesday the following February, Müller had given the last penny he had to the matron at one of the homes to buy the food she needed.

'We shall have to look to the Lord again for further supplies,' he said.

That afternoon a lady and gentleman were visiting the Wilson Street homes. At the Boys' home they met two ladies who were also on a visit. One of these ladies turned to the matron and said:

'Of course, you cannot carry on these institutions without a good stock of funds.'

Turning to the matron, the gentleman then said, 'Have you a good stock?'

The matron thought quickly. It was a firm rule at the homes that no-one ever told an inquirer how much money was in hand. During difficult times this would have been seen as begging. The matron replied:

'Our funds our deposited in a bank which cannot break.'

She noticed that tears came into the eyes of the lady who had asked the question. As he left, the gentleman gave the matron £5.

Next month, brother T was staying in Devon for a break. He passed on to a friend the latest Annual Report of the work in the homes. This friend read the report and then decided to pray that his sister would give some of her valuable jewellery towards the work at Wilson Street. Before long his prayer was answered, and Müller's helper returned from Devon with a heavy gold chain, a ring set with ten diamonds, a pair of gold bracelets and two pounds in money.

George Müller took the diamond ring, before

parting with it, and very neatly scratched the words JEHOVAH JIREH on a pane of glass in his room. The Hebrew words mean 'The Lord will provide'. Many times afterwards, until he left his home in Paul Street, his spirits were lifted as he caught sight of the words on the glass and remembered the remarkable way in which he came by the ring.

10: Up on the down

There were many times during the years which followed when money or supplies arrived at Wilson Street with only hours or even minutes to spare before the children sat down at table. Müller never changed his mind that neither he nor any member of his staff should ever appeal for funds.

One of the worst periods was the six months which ended in April 1842. For week after week, with only short periods of relief, the funds had been no more than sufficient. On Tuesday, April 12th, the need had never been greater. Since the previous Saturday less than fourteen shillings (70p) had been received at Wilson Street. Early in the morning, Müller knelt in prayer:

'Lord pity us! You know that we badly need some oatmeal, some new pairs of shoes, money for the repair of old shoes and to replenish our stores, and some money for new clothes for the children as well as a little money which is needed for some of the lady helpers. Please send some larger sums.'

Later that morning an envelope arrived from the East Indies: it contained one hundred pounds. Müller recorded, 'It is impossible to describe the real joy in God it gave me . . . I was not in the least surprised or excited when this donation came, for I took it as that which came in answer to prayer, and had been long looked for'.

In October 1845 Müller received a letter from a gentleman who lived in Wilson Street. Although the tone of the letter was friendly, the writer said that there were various ways in which he and his neighbours were 'inconvenienced' through the children's homes being in Wilson Street. He left it to Müller to decide what action to take.

As you might expect, Müller set aside several hours to pray and think about this problem. And then, a few days later, a friend of his – Robert Chapman of Barnstaple – arrived in Bristol. Müller decided to discuss the whole matter with Mr Chapman.

'I am not upset by the letter,' he told his friend, 'and do not disagree with much of what it says. It is true that the children are noisy, although it is only the noise that dear children naturally make when they are together. It is not the sort of noise for which I think they should be blamed or which I should try to stop.

'You know that I have now opened a fourth home,' Müller continued, 'and nearly one hundred and fifty children and staff now live in Wilson Street. I should love to have more than the single playground for the children to play in, and some gardens where the older children could work. I should like us to do all the laundry work on our own premises.

'A more invigorating spot closer to the country would be healthier for the children; and it would be nice for the teachers and staff to have somewhere to relax in a garden or walk in a field after hours.'

Robert Chapman seemed sympathetic.

'For some years.' Müller concluded, 'I have been looking for property in Bristol which would meet these needs but I have found none. The more I think and pray about it, the more I feel that God is calling me to build a brand new home which will have all the features I have discovered a children's home needs'.

Chapman was very much in favour of the idea and also told Müller:

'You must ask help from God to show you the plan, so that all may be according to the mind of God.'

At no time since the beginning of his children's work had their been more applications for admission to the homes, and Müller did not find it easy to refuse so many children a home. After a period when they prayed every morning about this possible new venture, George and Mary were satisfied that it was God's will. Their next step was to ask Him for the money they would need – at least £10,000.

Two months after Müller had received the letter from the Wilson Street resident, he was sent the first donation towards the new building: it was a gift of £1000 – the largest single donation he had ever received.

At about the same time, Mary's sister made a visit to London. There she met a Christian architect who was fascinated to hear of Müller's plans to build a new home.

'I should be delighted,' he told her, 'to draw up plans and superintend the building free of charge.'

Müller was naturally delighted with this news. The same month, he received another donation of £1000 towards the new building.

A few weeks later, he heard of some land which was for sale. It was high up on Ashley Down, in a bracing position on the north side of Bristol with long views eastwards towards Stapleton and north to Horfield. And yet it was within easy reach of the centre of Bristol and not too far from Bethesda Chapel.

Müller called at the home of the owner of the land and was told that he was at his place of business. On arrival there, he was told that the gentleman had just left, but that he would be at his home later in the evening.

'It is not God's will for us to meet today,' thought Müller and returned to Paul Street.

Next morning, Müller once again rang the front door bell of the fine house where the owner of the Ashley Down site lived.

'He is most anxious to see you,' Müller was told, 'and has asked that you be shown to his room as soon as possible.'

Müller was led to the gentleman's study.

'This morning I awoke at three o'clock and could not sleep again until five,' the owner of the land began. 'While I was lying awake I could think of nothing else but my land on Ashley Down and your enquiry which had been passed to me about the possibility of acquiring it for the building an Orphan House. At length I made up my mind that if you applied for it, I would sell it to you at £120 an acre instead of £200 which I was previously asking! '

'How good is the Lord!' thought Müller. He signed an agreement to buy nearly seven acres.

Next week the architect arrived from London and he and Müller visited the Ashley Down site.

'This site is most suitable,' he told Müller, 'on grounds of situation, drainage and water supply. '

When the plans were drawn up, Müller explained them to his staff.

'There will be room for three hundred children, one hundred and forty girls and eighty boys from eight upwards, and eighty infant boys aged up to seven. As you can see, there will be good accommodation for all our staff and teachers. Work will commence when the necessary funds have been received. '

In July, 1846, Müller received a single donation of £2000 for his new building; another of £1000 followed in December and a further £2000 in January 1847. The total received was now over £9000, and on August 19th the foundation stone of the new building was laid.

11: A kind of secret joy

'There is a visitor to see you,' Müller was told. It was the morning of Febrary 11th, 1849. The visitor introduced himself and explained the purpose of his visit.

'I had intended to leave you some money in my will, but I have now decided to give it to you during my life-time. I am anxious that not even my bank should know of my donation and I have therefore not written out a cheque. Here is the money in notes'.

After the visitor had left, Müller counted the money. It was two thousand pounds. Müller recorded, 'It is impossible to describe the real joy I had in God, when I received this sum. I was calm, not in the least excited, able to go on immediately with other work that came upon me . . .; but inexpressible was the delight which I had in God, who had thus given me the full answer to my thousands of prayers.' This gift brought the total he had received for the new building to nearly £16,000 and meant that the cost of building, furnishing and fitting out the home would be completely met.

In June, 1849, there was great excitement at Wilson Street. The children were to be moved to Ashley Down. They did not all move on the same day, but the first group arrived on the 18th. The boys looked particularly smart as a special gift had recently enabled Müller to buy each of them a new suit of clothes.

The sight of this large new building took their

breath away! And what a change it was from Wilson Street to hear the birds singing, to see cows grazing nearby, and to enjoy the view across the valley towards Stapleton. Once inside even the fresh paint and newly-polished woodwork smelt good, and the whole place was light and well aired.

After four days all the children, their teachers and the staff had moved into the new building. Some weeks later, one visitor to the 'New Orphan-House', as it was called, described what he had seen to a friend.

'We approached the house through a garden and, when the doors were opened, found ourselves in a very small hall. From there a stone staircase leads up into a large room in the central buildings. The room is a perfect square, with the four angles taken off by the width of the windows, which we found looked into large pitched play-courts, with covered sheds for the children's use in wet weather. In one court we saw some infant boys and girls who were toddling about under the care of two or three older girls.

'We were then taken to the Infants' Day Room, where we found a tribe of little things being looked after by a nurse. Ranged round one side of this room were a number of little basket beds, for use of the children when tired of play.

'In another room we found about half a dozen boys under the care of a lady busy darning socks. Another visitor in our party, an elderly lady, was most impressed by the boys' technique – "One thread up," she said, "and one thread down, is the very perfection of darning." '

'The washing-places we saw are furnished with baths and on the walls is hung each child's little bag with comb and hair-brush. The girls' hair is kept beautifully neat, such as we could fancy a mother's love had attended to.'

'Did the children seem happy?' the visitor's friend asked.

'Well I noticed that the children looked up cheerfully at the visitors, with a heart-smile on their young faces. I am sure that the spring of action in the house is love, and the spirit which rules is the law of kindness. Everyone engaged in the work seemed to be well fitted to his duties, and had a hearty unselfish love of the work for its own sake.'

When, at the beginning of 1851, Müller received a donation of three thousand pounds for the work he decided to speak to Mary about something which had been on his mind for a while.

'My dear,' he said, 'this donation is like a voice from heaven. I believe God is calling us to build another Orphan-House. Look, I have written down eight reasons against enlarging our work, with an answer to each objection and here I have written eight reasons for building a new home for seven hundred children.'

Mary read the sheet of paper carefully.

'Darling, how much do you think a new home would cost?' she asked.

'It would not be less than about £35,000. And do you know that the greatness of the sum required affords me a kind of secret joy; for the greater the difficulties to be overcome, the more would it be seen to the glory of God, how much can be done by prayer and faith'.

'I have no doubt that God can send us that amount, if we are sure that it is His will,' replied Mary. 'Let's pray about the matter together.'

The couple prayed about this new venture every day for five months. At the end of May, they were sure they knew God's will, and Müller announced that he intended to expand his work.

At first, few large sums were received. Part of the reason for this seems to have been a rumour which was circulating that Müller already had £30,000 in his building fund. Actually he had only just over £1000 in hand for the new venture but he refused to deny the rumour. This would have been to break his rule never to reveal the state of the funds. In any case, as he said to Mary:

'God knows that I have not £30,000 in hand. He can influence the minds of His dear children towards our intended Orphan-House, whatever rumours they may hear.

George and Mary knelt together in prayer.

'Lord, you know that the application list of children who need a home now numbers over six hundred names. You know how small an amount we have in hand compared with what is needed; but you know that we did not act rashly in this matter. In your mercy, sustain our faith and patience, and if it pleases you, speedily refresh our hearts by sending large sums, which we confidently expect.'

The prayer for faith and patience was answered, but the large sums did not come immediately. Come they did, though. The following spring, £1000 was received. And then, in January 1853, Müller received a promise that as the joint donation of several Christians, he was to receive £8100.

'See how precious it is to wait on God!' he said to Mary, beaming. The money was paid in four instalments.

The following January (1854) Müller received

another large donation of £5000, and yet another of nearly £6000 a year later.

By May 1855, the building fund was healthy enough to permit an immediate start on a second House on Ashley Down for four hundred girls. Four wells were sunk on the site and work commenced. As the building went up, more large donations were received.

12: When the south wind blew

'How does Mr Müller succeed in raising very large sums of money without ever appealing for funds?'

The question was often asked, and all sorts of ingenious explanations were offered. Some people said it was because he was a foreigner; some put it down to the novelty of the whole thing; others said Müller must have access to some secret treasure. The most popular explanation was that it was all the result of the Annual Reports of the work of the Homes.

Müller was amused by these suggestions, and in 1856 replied to them like this.

'My being a foreigner would surely be much more likely to hinder my being entrusted with such large sums, than to persuade donors to give. As to novelty procuring the money, the time is long gone by for this: it is now June 1856 and the work commenced in March 1834.

'As to the secret treasure to which I have access, there is more in this than people are aware of. For God's treasury is inexhaustible, and I have that (though that alone) to go to, and have indeed drawn out of it, simply by prayer and faith, more than £113,000 since the work began.'

What about the theory that the Annual Reports were the means by which the money was raised? Müller said:

'There is nothing unusual in writing Reports. This is done by public Institutions generally, but the constant complaint is that Reports are not read. Our Reports do not use powerful language, or appeal to feelings. They are simple statements of facts which are sent to donors, or to any individuals who wish to have or purchase them. If they produce results, which Reports generally do not, I can only ascribe it to the Lord.

'I do not doubt the Lord has again and again used the Reports as instruments in leading persons to help us. I ask the Lord day by day, and generally several times every day, to speak to the hearts of His dear children to help me out of the means with which He has entrusted them. And so I doubt not that the Lord again and again works by His Spirit in the hearts of those who have read or heard the Reports. But whether we are supplied with funds through the Reports or without them, in either case it is God who is working for us.'

Müller was able to open House 'No. 2' (as it became known) in November 1857. It lay immediately south of No. 1, at right angles to it, and had room for four hundred girls – two hundred infants and two hundred girls from eight upwards.

There were a lot of people who doubted whether Müller would be able to provide for seven hundred children, and the large staff which was now needed to look after them.

'One thing is certain,' they said, 'he will have to start appealing for funds. Prayer may work for a few small homes, but a work on this scale will need to be handled differently. We may be about to witness the most awful disaster.'

The rest of this book will reveal whether or not these sceptics were right.

Towards the end of November 1857, Müller was working in his room in house No.1 on Ashley Down. An assistant entered with some worrying news about the heating system (both new orphan-houses were centrally heated).

'The boiler which feeds the radiator in this building has a serious leak. It will be impossible for us to go through the winter unless it is repaired.'

'Do you know where the leak is?' Müller asked.

'No, we cannot discover where it is without taking down the brickwork. This would take several days, and I am afraid might do further damage to the boiler.'

'We must find a solution,' said Müller. 'I do not want the children – especially the youngest – to suffer from the cold. What are the possibilities? I suppose a new boiler would take many weeks to install.'

'Yes, certainly more than a month.'

'Can we introduce temporary gas stoves?' asked Müller.

'I have considered this, but there is not enough gas to spare from the lighting system to heat the large number of stoves which would be required. "Arnott's" stoves, too, will be unsuitable as they need long chimneys to remove fumes.'

'You have done well in investigating these possibilities,' said Müller, smiling. 'I am going to ask God to show us what to do. What I am *not* going to say is "I will trust God regarding it" and *do* nothing. That would not be faith at all. Something has to be done, and done quickly.'

That evening Müller spoke to Mary about this unexpected problem. After outlining the various possibilities he said:

'Money is not the problem. I would gladly spend hundreds of pounds to prevent the children suffering from the cold. The dilemma is to know just what to do and how to spend the money.'

George and Mary spent some time together asking God to help them make the right decision. At last they decided to have the brick-chamber opened to see the extent of the damage, and whether the boiler might be repaired, so as to carry them through the winter.

The following Wednesday was fixed as the date when the workmen were to come. The fire in the boiler would of course have to be put out while the repairs were under way. Unfortunately, five or six days before the agreed date arrived, a cold north wind set in. It was the first really cold weather of the winter. What was to be done? The repairs could not be put off and no-one wanted the children to freeze. Müller knelt in prayer.

'Dear God, please change this north wind into a south wind so that when the boiler is put out the children will not suffer from the cold.'

Then, as he was on his knees, he remembered some words in the Book of Nehemiah about how quickly the walls of Jerusalem were built, because 'the people had a mind to work'.

'Dear God,' he prayed, 'please give to the workmen a mind to work as you gave to the men who built the walls of Jerusalem in the days of Nehemiah.'

Until the Tuesday evening of the following week, the cold north wind blew.

Müller woke early on the Wednesday morning, the day the workmen were due to arrive to put the fire out. He walked out into the garden of his home in Paul Street. A warm south wind was blowing, just as he had prayed.

'How good is the Lord!' he said to Mary at breakfast. 'The weather is now so mild that no fire will be needed in the boiler.'

When Müller arrived on Ashley Down, the workmen had already begun to remove the brickwork. They quickly discovered where the leak was and a team from the boiler makers immediately began to repair the fault.

Müller left his room in No. 1 at half past eight that evening intending to walk home to Paul Street. But he was stopped at the main gate.

'Mr Müller,' said the gatekeeper. 'The head of the firm of boiler makers has arrived to see how the work is going and whether he can speed it up in any way.'

Müller went immediately to the cellar to meet the boss who was speaking to his men.

Turning to Müller, the boss said, 'The men will work late this evening, and come very early again tomorrow.'

'We would rather, sir,' said the foreman, 'work all night.'

Müller remembered the second part of his prayer. Who could doubt that God had given these men 'a mind to work'?

By the following morning the repair was completed and the leak stopped, though with great difficulty. The brickwork was put up again and the fire lit in the boiler.

And all the time, the warm south wind blew.

13: Stars in the sky

So far, there was no reason for the sceptics to be confirmed in their doubts. Müller was caring for seven hundred children on Ashley Down – not only feeding them, but employing teachers, nurses and other staff to look after the needs of the children and maintain the buildings.

What the doubters did not know was that Müller was now planning a further expansion of his work. Every day he received three or four new applications giving details of children who it was hoped could be admitted to the homes.

Most other orphanages were still very choosy in deciding who they would accept. Later in the century, as new homes were founded, they tended to follow Müller's example and accept all truly needy children. But in the 1850s many poor children still faced the grim prospect of being sent to a workhouse.

Müller and his assistants were particularly anxious to expand their work because of its educational value. Lots of children who had arrived at the homes, including many teenagers, had been quite unable to read. Müller's teachers taught them reading, writing, arithmetic, grammar, geography, English and world history, composition, singing, needlework and – for the girls – domestic science.

Some people actually criticised Müller for educating the children 'above their station'. They said he was robbing factories, mills and mines of labour, but he would not be put off. Instead, he employed a school inspector to maintain the standards at his own school on Ashley Down and also at the other schools which he ran.

In September 1858 Müller bought eleven and a half acres of land on the other side of the road from Nos. 1 and 2. He planned that his third home would be large enough to look after four hundred and fifty children. And even while this home was being built, he was thinking and praying about further expansion. He decided to build two more large homes on Ashley Down so that he would eventually be caring for over two thousand children.

While Müller now used frequently to receive large donations towards his building fund, there were still periods when money towards the day-to-day expenses only arrived just in time to meet the needs.

A little girl who witnessed one of these occasions was called Abigail Townsend. Abigail's father was a close friend of Müller and helped him in his Sunday School work.

One morning in 1861, Abigail was playing in Müller's garden on Ashley Down when he came and took her by the hand.

'Come, see what our Father will do,' he said to her.

He led her into the long dining-room. The plates, cups and bowls were on the table, but they were all empty. The children were standing waiting for breakfast.

'Children, you know we must be in time for school,' said Müller. Lifting his hand he prayed, 'Dear Father, we thank you for what you are going to give us to eat.'

There was a knock at the door. It was the baker.

'Mr Müller I couldn't sleep last night. Somehow I felt you didn't have bread for breakfast, and the Lord wanted me to send you some. So I got up at two o'clock and baked some fresh bread, and have brought it.'

Müller thanked the baker and said a short prayer, praising God for His care.

Then there was a second knock at the door. This time, it was the milkman.

'Mr Müller, my milk cart has broken down outside the orphanage. I should like to bring in all the cans of milk, so that I can empty my waggon and repair it.'

Fortunately, scrapes as narrow as this were rare. Naturally, the incident impressed Abigail immensely and she often said she wanted to be like George Müller.

Once at Paul Street, she said: 'I wish God would answer my prayers like He does yours, Mr Müller.'

'He will,' said Müller.

Taking Abigail on his knee, he repeated the promise 'If you believe, you will receive whatever you ask for in prayer' (Matthew 21:22).

'Now, Abbie,' he asked, 'what is it you want to ask God for?'

'Some wool.'

Müller held Abbie's hands together and said, 'Now, you repeat what I say: Please God, send Abbie some wool.'

Jumping down Abigail ran out into the garden to play. She had no doubt that the wool would come. Then suddenly the thought came to her that God might not know what kind of wool she wanted. She ran back to Müller.

'I want to pray again.'

'Not now, dear, I am busy.'

'But I forgot to tell God the colour I want.'

Taking her up on his knee again, Müller said, 'That's right, be definite, my child, now tell God exactly what you want.'

'Please God, send it wa-re-gated,' said Abigail who knew lots of long words but could not pronounce her 'v's'.

Next morning the postman delivered a parcel to the Townsend's house. It was addressed to Abigail, who opened it in great excitement. It contained several balls of variegated wool. Abigail's Sunday School teacher had remembered that her birthday was close but was unsure of the date. Knowing that Abigail was a keen knitter, she had bought some wool and sent it. She had not got the date right, but it was enough to teach the little girl that God hears and answers prayer.

Müller's third home was opened in March, 1862. It was the largest of the buildings he built on Ashley Down and it is still a familiar landmark in Bristol. The stone used for No. 3 (and all the other Ashley Down homes) had been quarried locally. A man who lived in Horfield told a friend:

'Whenever I feel doubts about the Living God creeping into my mind, I get up and look through the night at the many windows lit up on Ashley Down, gleaming out through the darkness like stars in the sky.'

With a waiting list now of nearly a thousand children, Müller was anxious that still more stars should shine on Ashley Down. For some years he had had his eye on a beautiful site on the same side of Ashley Down Road as Nos. 1 and 2, opposite No. 3. He prayed long and hard about this piece of land. When he was sure that God wanted him to have the land, he persuaded the owner of the land to accept £5500 instead of £7000 for it, and embarked on the final phase of his adventure of faith.

14: Ilfracombe encounter

In 1865, Müller was sixty. As usual on his birthday, the 27th September, there were special helpings of cake and an enormous apple dumpling for each child. A week's holiday was taken from school and many of the children went blackberry picking.

How did the man who had the care of so many appear to others? A farmer who met him walking up Ashley Hill said that he seemed like a gentleman of leisure and without a care. He added:

'The twenty-third Psalm seemed written on his face.'

Arthur Tappan Pierson, who knew Müller well at this period of his life, described him like this.

'He is tall and slim, and always neatly attired. He is very erect with a firm and strong step. If you saw him resting you might think his expression stern, but he has a smile which so often lights up his eyes that it has left its marks on the lines of his face. He has an air of authority and majesty which is combined with a simplicity which is such that even children feel at home with him. He has never lost his German accent and always speaks slowly and distinctly. He loves a joke which is clean and has no sting for others.

'Once at Ilfracombe he was climbing with his wife and some friends on the hills that overlook the sea. He walked on a little ahead of the others, sat down until they caught up, and then, just as they had sat down, he got up and said:

' "Well now, we've had a good rest, let us go on." '

Müller loved Ilfracombe. On another visit there he was returning with Mary and Lydia from a climb up Capstone Hill. Two men approached them.

'Please excuse me,' one of them said, 'aren't you Mr Müller?'

'I am.'

'I have to give you some money for the orphans.'

Müller pointed to a nearby bench. 'Sit down,' he said, 'so that we can talk further.'

'I live near M,' said the man. 'I am a businessman, and a Christian. Recently I read one of your reports. I could not believe that you raised your money simply through prayer, but I could not stop thinking about it. Then, I heard about a property which was about to be sold. I decided I should like to buy it, if it were sold reasonably. I looked at it and had it valued. It was worth £300. Then I said to myself, "Let's see if God is really with Mr Müller. If I get this property for £100, I will give Mr Müller £100."

'I then instructed a person to bid for me at the auction where this property was sold. But I was so curious to see whether God really would act for you in this, that I set off to the place where the auction was to see what happened. When I arrived I discovered that the property had been sold to me for £100. I was amazed.

'Then I began to reflect on the principles on which you act and to wonder that as a Christian I or anyone else should dare to call in question what you say about answers to prayer; the more I think about it, the more I see how right it is to come to God for all we need and trust Him for everything.

'I then decided I wanted to pass the money on to you and called yesterday at your home in Bristol. And now, here we are at Ilfracombe, and I have met you in person.'

'Well,' said Müller, 'I am not surprised that God

worked for me at the auction, for I look to him every day for answers to prayer. I often get donations from complete strangers and recently had a letter from a lawyer in M about one of his clients who wanted to leave a legacy of £1000 for the children. I don't know anybody in M, nor do I know the name of the individual who proposes to leave this £1000.'

'About this legacy,' replied the businessman, 'I can tell you something. After I had got this property, and saw how wrong I had been in looking so sceptically on your work, as if there were no reality in prayer, I decided on helping you further. I have made my will and left you £1000 for the children.'

An hour later, this one-time sceptic called at Müller's lodgings with a cheque for £100.

In 1859 Müller's friend and fellow-worker from their Teignmouth days, Henry Craik, had called to see his doctor.

'You have a weak heart,' Craik was told.

His condition grew more serious, and Müller often visited him at his bedside. Müller remembered a visit in January 1866. After he had kissed his old friend, he saw that he was too weak to talk, and had made ready to go.

'Sit down,' said Henry to Müller and Mrs Craik. Craik looked at them both but was unable to speak. After a while Müller left. It was their last meeting. Both men had been Christians for over forty years.

Huge crowds gathered at Bethesda Chapel for Craik's funeral. Müller had now to work on without the benefit of Henry's wise advice and interest.

On Guy Fawkes' Day 1868, the fourth Ashley

Down home was opened; and the fifth and last in January 1870. Müller was now caring for some two thousand children plus a large staff and his vast expansion programme on Ashley Down was complete.

He certainly couldn't sit back and put his feet up. The children had to be fed and clothed; their clothes had to be washed and repaired. Buying new shoes and boots cost hundreds of pounds. If the children were ill, there was extra expense.

Each year, hundreds of new children arrived on Ashley Down and needed new clothes; all those who left were also fitted out and their travelling expenses paid. Each boy was provided with three suits of clothes, and those who went out as apprentices had a premium paid to their masters which was equal to another year's support.

Think of the expense of maintaining the five large Ashley Down houses. There were more than seventeen hundred large windows and over five hundred rooms to be painted, white-washed and repaired. Thousands of articles of linen and furniture had to be repaired or replaced.

The large staff included a school inspector, matrons, teachers, medical officers, nurses, domestics, and Müller's assistants. All their salaries had to be paid.

The cost of all this came to nearly £30,000 a year, and was met, as Müller used to say, by 'looking to the infinitely rich One for everything'.

This meant an immense amount of work for Müller. But he did not do it alone. Every morning he got up at half-past six, read his Bible and prayed to God until a quarter to eight, and then began to go through his correspondence. At ten o'clock, 9 assistants joined him in his room to receive their instructions for the day. His other helper was his wife.

Mary Müller was the ideal wife for the director of five large children's homes.

'My darling,' Müller often used to say to her, 'God himself singled you out for me, as the most suitable wife I could possibly wish to have had. I never saw you at any time since you became my wife, without my being delighted to see you. Do you think there is a couple in Bristol, or in the world, happier than we are?'

Müller believed that one of the secrets of their happiness was the time they spent praying together. They would devote time to this every morning, and often again after lunch. If things were especially difficult they would meet again several times during the afternoon. Every evening, in good times as well as bad, they set aside their last hour at Ashley Down for prayer. During these periods, they would bring perhaps fifty or more different items to God.

Mary spent every day, except Sundays, on Ashley Down and always paid particular attention to the sick children. It was also her responsibility to order hundreds of thousands of yards of blankets, linen and other materials for Ashley Down use. She examined all the account books every month and checked hundreds of bills. It used to be said that if anyone made a mistake, Mary would be sure to find them out.

15: Something to hold on to

William Ready was born in a London workhouse in January 1860. Both his parents died when he was five and he was left an orphan together with his nine brothers and sisters.

William left the workhouse and began to sleep in dustbins or under railway arches. Sometimes he was so hungry that he gladly ate pieces of orange peel and even cigar ends. As he grew older, he began to earn money by singing comic songs in pubs and by carrying fruit and vegetables at Covent Garden market. Often his feet and hands were frostbitten.

At the age of twelve, he was rescued by a London City Missioner who arranged for him to be sent to Ashley Down. William didn't take kindly to this and when he saw the five enormous buildings he longed to return to the bright lights of London.

He was given a bath, and dressed in corduroy trousers, a blue waistcoat, jacket and white collar. He never forgot the day when he was first shown into the dining-hall, and some years later described the experience like this:

'The boys gathered round me like flies round a sugar basin and they began to pinch me and pull my hair. The bell rang and we passed to our places. For the first time in my life I was not feeling hungry. Oh! to go back to my old haunts, to the rush of cabs and buses! Two slices of bread and treacle were set before me on a little tin plate but I could not touch them. A boy said to me, "Don't you want your tea?" I answered, "No!" The boys on either side of me soon finished my share.'

Next morning, at breakfast, the tables were laid with bowls of porridge. William didn't give the boys the chance of asking if he wanted his food, for his appetite had returned. At this breakfast, he heard the Bible read for the first time.

A reading lesson followed, and William's master discovered that he didn't know the letters of the alphabet. In a few months, however, he learned to read well. He was taught the gospel story and memorised portions of the Bible.

William was popular with the other boys, and started a class at which he taught acrobatic tricks he had learned in London. His master discovered that he had charged those who could afford to pay a penny postage stamp a week for his instruction. As the boys had paid without any pressure from William, no more was said.

On another occasion, William was not so lucky. He led a party of boys on an invasion of the masters' dining-room in the dark to demolish the remains of their evening meal. He was caught and caned; but after applying the stick the master took pity on him and gave him some sweets.

One morning in 1876, after four years on Ashley Down, William was called out of his class.

'How would you like to be a flour miller, Ready?' he was asked.

'I would, yes, Sir,' William answered not knowing what the job involved in the slightest.

He was measured and provided with his three suits of clothes. Then his master told him:

'Mr Müller would like to see you.'

William knocked at the door of the director's room in No. 3 house, and waited. Müller called him in and, smiling at him, put half a crown into his left hand and a Bible in his right.

'You can hold tighter with your right hand than with your left, can you not?'

'Yes, Sir.'

'Well, my lad.' said Müller, 'hold to the teaching of that book and you will always have something for your left hand to hold.'

Müller asked William to kneel, put his hand on his head, and prayed that God would look after him. Then, helping him to his feet, he gave him a verse from the Bible.

'Trust in the Lord and do good; so you shall dwell in the land and truly you shall be fed. Goodbye, my boy, goodbye!'

William said later:

'I left Ashley Down with my Bible, my clothes and half a crown. But what was best of all, was the priceless blessing of George Müller's prayers'.

William travelled to Newton Abbot in Devon and was met by a man with a long beard and a straw-hat.

'Are you William Ready?'

'Yes, Sir.'

'Well, I am your master, or your father if you like. Get into the trap, my son.'

William Perryman chatted cheerily to William as they drove through lovely country lanes to Chagford. Perryman was a Christian, and early on in his apprenticeship, William himself was converted to Christ. Much later, he moved to New Zealand and became a popular preacher.

Looking back on his years on Ashley Down he wrote:

'I can see now that it was just the place for me and what a blessing it was that I was sent there. If my own children were left orphans I could wish for nothing better than that they should be trained and cared for at Müller's'.

A well-dressed gentleman with a neat beard arrived at Ashley Down.

'I should like to speak to Mr Müller,' he told the gatekeeper.

The gentleman was escorted to the Director's room, and introduced himself.

'I am Charles Dickens. I have been interested to hear of the work you are doing and have come to see your homes for myself.'

Since the publication of *Oliver Twist* at the time of the opening of the first Wilson Street home, Dickens had written many popular books and had become famous. He had retained his interest in the care of children and had helped to raise money for the Hospital for Sick Children in London.

Müller called for an assistant and handed him a bunch of keys.

'Please show Mr Dickens around any parts of the five houses he wishes to see.'

The tour began with a visit to one of the school rooms where a class of thirteen year old girls was receiving a lesson in English grammar. They were dressed in blue-checked gingham pinafores and their shoulder length hair was held back with velvet ribbon bands.

The assistant whispered a few words to the class teacher who gasped in amazement. Then she turned to the children.

'How many of you have read *Pickwick Papers*?'
Several hands went up.

'And who is the author of that book?'

'Charles Dickens, Miss.'

'This, children, is Mr Dickens.'

Dickens stayed for a while to hear some of the children read and to look at their exercise books. The teacher explained with some pride that the children had recently sat for their annual examination and that the average mark had been 91.1 per cent.

Next, Dickens met some older boys returning from a visit to Bristol. He noticed their uniforms – navy-blue serge jackets and waistcoats with white starched collars, brown corduroy trousers, and peak caps. He wondered whether looking identical worried them, but they seemed cheerful enough.

It was lunch-time, and Dickens was shown into the large dining room.

'It's og again today,' one of the children said.

Dickens wanted to know what 'og' was. He was told that it was mutton, but no-one seemed to know how it had acquired this strange name. Then he heard one of the children ask his neighbour to pass the 'toke'. Dickens was puzzled again, but this time there was an explanation.

'A favourite grace on Ashley Down,' Müller's assistant said, 'goes like this. "We thank thee Lord for these tokens of thy love." And so bread is toke. It's as simple as that.'

After the main course, the children tucked in either to bananas or oranges, and there seemed to be almost no limit to the quantity of fruit they were allowed. It was explained to Mr Dickens that a load of free fruit had been delivered to Ashley Down from the port of Bristol, and that this was not unusual at a time of surplus.

A group of children told Dickens that the following day was the date of the annual summer outing to Pur Down. Each of them would set off armed with either a pink or blue cotton bag filled with sweets and biscuits to eat on the journey. If the weather looked doubtful, there would be one cotton umbrella between two. The picnic would arrive on

Pur Down in large hampers, and the children of the five houses would be able to mix as they pleased.

'And don't forget the fire balloons,' said the youngest. Mr Dickens was informed that the outing would end with the launching of five fire balloons, one for each house.

It is said that Dickens made his visit to Ashley Down because he had heard criticism of the running of the homes, but that he went away entirely reassured.

16: Looking for the answer

Mary Müller seemed to others to be doing her work on Ashley Down much as usual. But she knew otherwise: for some time she had not been sleeping well and now there was something more. She had suddenly developed a pain across the lower part of her back and in her right arm.

It was January, 1870, and Mary was seventy-two. Dr Josiah Pritchard looked grave as he gave Müller his diagnosis.

'She must go to bed and a fire is to be lit in her room. It is rheumatic fever.'

Everything possible was done to make Mary comfortable. Müller was broken-hearted but trusted that God would do what was right. The day after receiving the doctor's verdict he sat alone in Mary's room on Ashley Down. He could not remember being there on his own before. On the wall was a day-to-day calendar. He read the text for the day which was from Psalm 119:75.

'I know, O Lord, that your judgments are righteous, and in faithfulness you have afflicted me. All this is according to your love, and whatever the issue, all will be well.'

Underneath the text were the words 'My times are in your hands' (Psalm 31:15).

'Yes, my Father,' thought Müller, 'the times of my darling wife are in your hands. You will do the very best thing for her and for me, whether in life or death. If it may be, raise up yet again my precious wife, you are able to do it, though she is so ill; but however you deal with me, help me to continue to be perfectly satisfied with your holy will.'

Later in the week, Dr Pritchard instructed Müller that every two hours through the night he was to give Mary either tea or a little wine in water. Each time he did so, he prayed with her.

On the Saturday night Mary's pains grew worse. Müller spent most of the night trying to comfort her as best he could.

On the Sunday, Josiah Pritchard arrived and told Müller:

'All hope of recovery is now gone.'

Pritchard left and Müller took Mary's hand in his.

'The Lord Jesus is coming for you,' he said.

'He will come soon!' Mary replied.

Early in the afternoon, Mary found it difficult to swallow her medicine and her speech became indistinct. As he sat quietly beside Mary, George noticed that 'her dear bright eyes were set'. He called Lydia and Mary's sister and told them that Mary was dying.

They sat and watched her until at 4:20, Sunday, February 6th 1870, Mary died. Müller fell to his knees.

'Thank you, dear Father, for releasing our darling Mary from her suffering. Thank you for taking her to yourself. Please help and support us at this time.'

George and Mary had been married for forty years. Müller conducted the funeral service himself. Before preaching the sermon, he sat in the vestry repeating over and over again:

'Oh Mary, my Mary!'

He took as his text, 'You are good, and what you do is good', from Psalm 119:68. He described how good God had been in giving him such a marvellous wife. He spoke of how he missed her more and more each day and how he saw the great loss her death had been to the children. And yet he concluded by acknowledging that God had done that which was good in taking her to be with Himself.

'Without an effort, my inmost soul habitually joys in the joy of that loved departed one. Her happiness gives joy to me. My dear daughter and self would not have her back, were it possible to produce it by the turn of the hand. God Himself has done it, we are satisfied with Him.'

These were brave words, but in the months to come George felt the loss deeply. He recorded that while he sought to praise God and be satisfied with Him, his 'earthly joy was all but gone'.

Meanwhile the massive work of caring for two thousand children and employing hundreds of staff continued. The money needed for this operation was raised simply by the prayer of faith. And Müller was so confident that God would meet his needs that he did not put every pound he received to the work on Ashley Down.

During his life he was given one and a half million pounds towards his work for God. It is difficult to believe – but true – that of this he devoted nearly half a million pounds to causes other than his children's work in Bristol.

Back in the 1830s he had given the name Scriptural Knowledge Institution to an organisation which supported a range of activities in addition to his own care of children. Under the umbrella of this Institution (which still flourishes today), Müller founded and supported schools in many countries throughout the world; circulated thousands of Bibles, Testaments, tracts and books; and sent over £260,000 to missionaries all over the world. During the 1870s he sent £10,000 abroad every year to nearly two hundred missionaries.

Müller never appealed for all this money: he never organised a sponsored walk or arranged a special fund raising event. What would he have thought of these devices? We do not know: he did not criticise the way that other charities conducted their affairs. All we know is that he saw his as a special work – established to demonstrate that there is reality in the things of God. Prayer works and, for him, this was enough.

Müller often preached about prayer. Once, at Bethesda Chapel, he took as his text Matthew 7:7–8, 'Ask and it will be given you; seek and you will find; knock and the door will be opened to you. For everyone who asks receives; he who seeks finds; and to him who knocks, the door will be opened.'

People listened eagerly to what he said, because here was a man who didn't just talk about prayer. He put it into practice and got results.

He said that there were a number of conditions on which successful prayer depended. First, we must ask for those things which are according to God's will; second, we must remember the warning in Psalm 66:18 that if we have sin in our hearts God will not hear us. Then, we must believe that God *wants* to answer our prayers and wait patiently for the answer.

To show the importance of patience in prayer, he ended his sermon with the following remarkable story.

'In November 1844 I began to pray for the conversion of five individuals. I prayed every day without one single intermission, whether sick or in health, on the land or on the sea, and whatever the pressure of my engagements might be. Eighteen months elapsed before the first of the five was converted. I thanked God, and prayed on for the others.

'Five years elapsed, and then the second was converted. I thanked God for the second, and prayed on for the other three. Day by day I continued to pray for them, and six years more passed before the third was converted. I thanked God for the three, and went on praying for the other two.

'These two remain unconverted. The man to whom God in the riches of His grace has given tens of thousands of answers to prayer, in the self-same hour or day on which they were offered, has been praying day by day for nearly thirty-six years for the conversion of these two individuals, and yet they remain unconverted; for next November it will be thirty-six years since I began to pray for their conversion. But I hope in God, I pray on, and look for the answer.'

Of the two people still unconverted at the time of this sermon, one became a Christian before Müller died and the other a few years later.

17: Preacher to royalty

For some years, one of Müller's most valuable helpers in the work on Ashley Down had been Mr James Wright. George had often prayed that God would fit Wright to succeed him as Director of the homes.

Wright was widely respected and loved. People used to say that the radiant smile on his face showed that peace and joy ruled his heart. He was very fond of music and his beautiful bass voice was a familiar sound at Bethesda Chapel.

After some initial hesitation, Wright agreed to become co-director with Müller of the work which he had built up, including the range of activities run by the Scriptural Knowledge Institution further afield than Ashley Down. It was understood that if Müller died, James Wright would succeed him.

One morning, some eighteen months after taking up his job, James Wright stood in Müller's room at No. 3 with an embarrassed expression on his face.

'I should like to marry Lydia,' he said.

Wright's first wife had died some years earlier, and this request came as a complete surprise to Müller. We do not know how he replied, but he recorded in his diary:

'I knew no one, to whom I could so willingly entrust this my choicest earthly treasure.'

They were married at Bethesda Chapel in November 1871. Wright was forty-five and Lydia thirty-nine. Wright later described their life together as a time of 'unbroken felicity'.

Later that same November, Müller was at Bethesda again for another wedding.

This time, he was the bridegroom.

It was nearly two years since Mary had died. As with every step Müller took, the decision to marry again was only made after much prayer. His bride was Susannah Sangar, whom he had known for more than twenty-five years.

The chief feature of Müller's second marriage was a remarkable series of preaching tours. In seventeen years, the couple travelled about two hundred thousand miles to thirty countries. Susannah loved travel and made an ideal companion for Müller who was seventy when the tours began (in 1875). The second Mrs Müller was twenty years younger than her husband and acted both as nurse and secretary. She made sure that the tours were not all work and no play: despite George's numerous preaching engagements they took time to visit tourist attractions and places of historic interest.

Susannah never spoke in public but helped Müller distribute thousands of Bibles, testaments and tracts in many different languages. She often spoke privately to people about the Christian gospel.

The year Müller began his preaching tours was also the year in which the famous American evangelists Moody and Sankey conducted a successful gospel campaign in Britain. Moody had said there were three men in England he longed to meet: one of them was George Müller. He duly visited Bristol and was uplifted by Müller's unshakeable faith in God. The first tours were confined to Britain and Müller said that one of his special aims was to follow up the work done by Moody and Sankey by encouraging young Christians.

Wherever Müller went, in country after country, he attracted large audiences to hear him. Sometimes hundreds of people had to be turned away because there was simply no room left after galleries had been filled and all available extra chairs had been commissioned. Müller's method was simply to expound a short passage from the Bible taking great care that his points were well understood and to illustrate them with frequent stories. Congregations would listen spellbound to accounts of God's provision for the children on Ashley Down or of Müller's own answers to prayer. But it was Christ, not himself, who Müller sought to proclaim.

A bronzed, weather-beaten man, the captain of a merchant vessel sat in the immense Victoria Hall in Liverpool. Years previously he had been a child on Ashley Down. Now he sat with five or six thousand others and listened to Müller preach. As, for the first time, he began to understand the motive of Müller's life he wept and was converted. He was one of many in years to come.

Müller's tours often brought him into contact with famous people. He did not seek this attention, but as he received invitations from Presidents and Princesses he felt that God was calling him to this special form of service from time to time.

At Stuttgart, in 1877, he was sent for by the Queen of Württemberg and answered Her Majesty's questions about his work in Bristol. At Darmstadt, that same year, Müller spoke at a series of drawing room meetings at the home of the court preacher. Princess Karl (Mother of Prince Louis of Hesse, husband of Princess Alice of England), and Princess von Battenberg shook Müller warmly by the hand, and followed up his talk with eager questions.

When Müller preached in Berlin, Count Bismarck (cousin of the famous Prince) came one hundred and twenty-five miles on purpose to hear him preach. He had read the *Narratives of the Lord's dealings with George Müller*.

'Your *Narratives* have been a great blessing to my soul,' he told Müller.

But at Dusseldorf, Müller was equally delighted to meet and try to help the City Missioner. The gentleman was in some distress.

'I have six sons and have been praying without success for their conversion for many years. Tell me what I should do?'

'*Continue* to pray for your sons,' Müller replied, 'and *expect* an answer to your prayer, and you will have to praise God.'

Six years later Müller met the missioner again.

'Two months after you left,' he told Müller, 'five of my sons were converted. And now the sixth is thinking seriously about the truth of the gospel.'

Müller rejoiced.

Müller made several long visits to the United States and preached to thousands of Americans. There is a fascinating incident associated with his first visit. The couple set off in August 1877 aboard the *Sardinian*.

As the ship approached Newfoundland the weather turned cold and a thick fog formed. The ship's speed was reduced and a serious delay seemed inevitable.

The captain had been on the bridge for twenty-four hours when George Müller appeared at his side.

'Captain, I have come to tell you I must be in Quebec by Saturday afternoon.'

'It is impossible.'

'Very well,' said Müller, 'if your ship cannot take

me, God will find some other way – I have never broken an engagement for fifty two years. Let us go down into the chart-room and pray.'

'Mr Müller,' said the captain, 'do you know how dense this fog is?'

'No, my eye is not on the density of the fog, but on the living God, who controls every circumstance of my life.'

'Very well, follow me.'

In the chart-room, Müller knelt down and asked God to lift the fog. When he had finished the captain was about to pray, but Müller put his hand on his shoulder and told him not to.

'First, you do not believe He will, and second, I believe He has, and there is no need whatever for you to pray about it. Captain, I have known my Lord for fifty-two years, and there has never been a single day that I have failed to get an audience with the King. Get up, captain, and open the door, and you will find the fog is gone.'

The captain walked across to the door and opened it.

The fog had lifted and the *Sardinian* reached Quebec on time. An evangelist later described the captain as 'one of the most devoted men I ever knew'.

18: A summons in St Petersburg

'9.30 am, January 10th, 1878: Meet Mr and Mrs George Müller from Bristol, England.'

It was a fairly routine entry in the United States President's diary, but an appointment which George and Susannah would not forget. The President received them warmly, and spent over half an hour in conversation with Müller, before Mrs Hayes conducted the couple through the White House.

A gruelling three weeks in Washington followed with Müller often preaching twice a day, but they found time to climb to the top of the domb on the Capitol building and admire the view.

From Washington, they travelled up to Salem in the Allegheny mountains where Müller preached to crowded congregations at the Lutheran church. On one evening the church was packed with students from local colleges and the seating arrangements on that evening give a fairly typical picture of Müller's engagements on his American tours. Many sat on the platform from which Müller spoke; the gallery was full with a back row standing on forms, their heads near the ceiling. At the front of the gallery, the most daring members of the congregation sat with their legs dangling above the pews below them. Many others stood closely packed together at the entrance throughout Müller's ninety-five minute address!

'You are the first person who has found the way to her heart for these nine years,' a Californian woman wrote to Müller. 'She says she would not have lost that sermon for a hundred dollars.' For nine years, the writer's daughter had been dabbling in the occult: as a result of Müller's sermon she had committed her life to Christ.

Müller received as eager hearings on the west coast as on the east and he seems even on that side of the continent to have become something of a household name. Driving through the Yosemite Valley, a stage-waggon carrying the Müllers and ten others passengers had one day to slow down to allow a smaller waggon carrying a man and woman to pass. Suddenly the woman jumped to her feet.

'Is that George Müller?'

'It is.'

'Then I must shake hands with you, sir. I have read your *Life of Trust*, and have been greatly blessed by it.'

Müller obliged.

'Pray for me!' shouted the woman as their journey continued.

During their tours of Europe, the Müllers were able to visit some of the schools supported by the Scriptural Knowledge Institution. One such was in a poor district of Barcelona. Müller spoke slowly to the children while the headmaster translated.

'My dear children, I love you all very much, and pray for you every day. I long from my inmost soul to meet everyone of you in Heaven; but in order, that you may go to that happy place, as poor, lost, guilty sinners, you must put your trust in the blessed Lord Jesus Christ, who was punished in our room and stead; for His blood alone can cleanse us from our sins.'

After Müller had told the children about Ashley Down, a pretty little girl with black hair and bright eyes stood on a form and recited Psalm 128.

While in the south of France, at Menton, Müller preached in a hall belonging to the Free Church of Scotland. Its doors and windows were left open, and several people sat outside on a balcony and listened to Müller in the spring sunshine. It was March, 1879, and among the little balcony audience was an Englishman in his middle forties, there for the benefit of his health: Charles Haddon Spurgeon.

Several times George and Susannah drove out with Spurgeon. One afternoon they took the Turin road leading to Castiglione, and winding slowly up a hill in an open carriage amid magnificent scenery Spurgeon said:

'When in the midst of landscapes such as these from the crown of my head to the sole of my foot, I feel as though I could burst out into one song of praise.'

We don't know whether he did so, or whether, if he did, Müller accompanied him. We do know that Spurgeon's son said that his father was better able to 'trust and not be afraid' after he had spent time with Müller.

At St Petersburg, in Russia, the Müllers were invited to stay with Princess Lieven, whom Mrs Müller described as 'a beloved sister in the Lord'. The Müllers declined this invitation at first but eventually gave in to the Princess's persistent pressure.

Drawing room meetings were highly popular amongst St Petersburg society at this time, and Müller spoke at a large number of them. One Friday evening during their eleven week stay with the Princess, the Müllers were startled to hear that unexpected visitors had arrived at the mansion. It was the police, with a summons for Müller to appear next morning before their chief officer.

'You are charged with holding meetings with translation into Russian without permission from the Minister of the Interior.'

The charge however was not a serious one and had arisen out of a misunderstanding. Müller was treated with courtesy but forbidden to hold any further meetings at the home of one of Russia's most active and influential Christians, Colonel Paschkoff. Some years later Paschkoff was exiled to Siberia by Tsar Alexander III.

One of Müller's later tours took him to Australia, New Zealand and India. At Calcutta Müller worked very hard, preaching many times in heat which was intense even for India. He was now (in 1889) 83 years old and he was warned by a doctor to leave Calcutta as soon as possible. The couple caught a northbound train, but it was almost too late. Müller was taken quite seriously ill and Susannah thought he was about to die. However the train arrived at the shores of the Ganges and she managed to get her husband aboard a steam ferry. The night breezes blowing across the river revived him.

They then caught a comfortable train bound for Siligari at the foot of the Himalayas. From Siligari, a steam tram-carriage took them up into the hills, and at a boarding house outside Darjeeling with fine views over snow-covered mountains Müller regained his health.

Within a few days, Müller resumed his Indian tour with a busy programme of meetings, until at Jubbulpore, he was handed a telegram from his son-in-law, James Wright. Müller's only child

Lydia Wright had died at the age of 57 after a short illness. The news was a heavy blow and the Müllers returned to England by the first suitable steamer.

The final preaching tour took the Müllers to Germany, Switzerland and Italy and lasted for nearly two years. When he arrived home, in the spring of 1892, Müller was 87. Hundreds of thousands of people had heard him preach and his name had become a byword for faith in many parts of the world.

19: Men's hearts moved

In January, 1894, Susannah died suddenly from a stroke after she and George had been married for twenty-three years. She was seventy-three. After a total of over sixty-two years married life, Müller naturally spoke of his great loneliness. But he spoke, too, of his practice of 'admiring the Lord's kindness' to him in so many ways throughout his life and of his gratitude that Susannah was now happy in God's presence.

Müller gave up his home in Paul Street and moved into a simply furnished suite of rooms in No. 3 House on Ashley Down.

On his ninetieth birthday, in September 1895, a presentation was made to him in Bethesda Chapel. During his speech of thanks he said that his voice was stronger than it had been seventy years earlier (when the army had rejected him on health grounds) and that he felt his mental powers to be as good as ever. He continued to play his normal part in running the children's homes and regularly took part in Sunday morning services at Bethesda, Alma Road and Stokes Croft Chapels.

Early in the summer of 1897 Charles Parsons visited Müller in his study at No. 3. Müller welcomed him with a cordial handshake.

'Have you always found the Lord faithful to His promises?' Parsons asked.

'Always,' replied Müller. 'He has never failed me. For nearly seventy years every need in connection with this work has been supplied. The orphans, from the first until now, have numbered nine thousand five hundred, but they have never wanted a meal. Never! Hundreds of times we have commenced the day without a penny in hand, but our Heavenly Father has sent supplies by the moment they were actually required. There never was a time when we had no wholesome meal.

'During all these years I have been enabled to trust in God, in the Living God, and in Him alone. £1,400,000 have been sent to me in answer to prayer. We have wanted as much as £50,000 in one year, and it has all come by the time it has been really needed.

'No man on earth can say that I have ever asked him for a penny. We have no committees, no collectors, no voting and no endowments. All has come in answer to believing prayer.

'My trust has been in God alone; He has many ways of moving the hearts of men to help us all over the world.'

During his talk, Charles Parsons asked Müller whether he had ever thought of saving for himself.

He never forgot Müller's response. He described later how the old man had 'looked for several moments into my face with an earnestness that seemed to penetrate through my very soul.' Müller then unbuttoned his coat and took from his pocket an old-fashioned purse. He gave it to Parsons.

'All I am possessed of is in that purse – every penny! Save for myself! Never! When money is sent to me for my own use I pass it on to God. As much as £1,000 has thus been sent at one time, but I do not regard these gifts as belonging to me; they belong to Him, Whose I am, and Whom I serve. Save for myself! I dare not save; it would be dishonouring to my loving, gracious, all-bountiful Father.'

Parsons spent an hour with Müller. Once during this time there was a knock at the door. Müller opened it to one of the children, a fair haired little girl.

'My dear,' he said, 'I cannot attend to you just now. Wait a while, and I will see you.'

Someone once asked Müller what was the secret of his life of service for God. He replied:

'There was a day when I died, utterly died; died to George Müller, his opinions, preferences, tastes and will – died to the world, its approval or censure – died to the approval or blame even of my brethren and friends – and since then I have studied only to show myself approved unto God.'

20: Bright prospect

In his nineties, Müller rarely left Bristol. One exception was the summer of 1897 when he agreed to take a few weeks rest at Bishopsteignton – a village in Devon which he had got to know well seventy years earlier as a young pastor in Teignmouth.

His hosts were determined that his visit should be as restful as possible. However, to their consternation, a few hours after his arrival he asked:

'What opportunity is there here for service for the Lord?'

'But you have come to rest!'

'But now that I am free from my usual work on Ashley Down, I must be occupied in some other way in God's service.'

Try as they would, Müller's hosts could not persuade him to take life easy. They therefore arranged meetings for him to speak at Bishopsteignton and Teignmouth.

Müller returned to Bristol and resumed his normal workload. The leaves on Ashley Down turned golden and then fell: autumn gave way to winter. Despite the cold, Müller still ventured out to preach. Speaking once that winter in Old Market Street Chapel it was said that he seemed full of the Holy Spirit.

'While all things change here below,' he said, 'the precious Jesus our friend, is "the same yesterday, and today, and forever". What He was when He walked through Judea, Samaria and Galilee, He is now – His heart full of tenderness, of pity, of compassion.

'Though you be the greatest, the oldest, the most

hardened sinner, though you have sinned again and again, if you now trust in Christ, you will for His sake be forgiven, for there is power in the blood of Christ to take away the greatest sins.

'Oh the blessedness of being a disciple of the Lord Jesus! I am a happy old man! I walk about my room, and I say, "Lord Jesus, I am not alone, for you are with me. I have buried my wives and my children, but you are left. I am never lonely or desolate with you and with your smile, which is better than life itself!" '

The presence with him every day of his Saviour: this was a reality which comforted Müller in his loneliness. But as spring approached in 1898 another thought, too, seemed increasingly to dominate his mind. It was the prospect of an eternity spent with Christ. He spoke of this at Alma Road Chapel on the first Sunday morning in March.

'Oh the bright, glorious prospect which we poor, miserable sinners have through faith in Christ Jesus! And at last taken home to be forever with the Lord, and to see that lovely One who laid down His life for us, ourselves being permitted to kiss His feet, ourselves being permitted to kiss His hands! Oh the precious prospect that awaits us!'

He spent the afternoon with a friend, Benjamin Perry.

'How very kind and good the Lord has been to me,' he told Perry. 'Now in my ninety-third year I am still without rheumatism, or an ache or pain, and I can still do my ordinary work at the Orphan-Houses with as much comfort to myself as seventy years ago.'

And so he did, working as usual at his desk at

No. 3 on the Monday and Tuesday. At breakfast on the Wednesday he said to James Wright:

'This morning when I got up, I felt weak and had to rest three times while I dressed.'

'Then in future,' suggested Wright, 'you must have an attendant to help you in the mornings.'

'After tomorrow,' said Müller.

Later in the day, he told Wright:

'I feel quite myself again.'

That evening, March 9, after leading the usual weekly prayer meeting in No. 3, he climbed the stairs to his bedroom. A few seconds later, a young student teacher, then living in No. 3, bounded up the stairs cheerily singing a chorus as she ran.

At the top of the first flight of stairs, she realised that Müller was ahead – standing quite still outside his bedroom. He waited until she reached him and then said:

'I am so glad to see you so happy, but you must not run up the stairs two at a time, you may hurt yourself'.

The young teacher watched as Müller opened his bedroom door and retired for the night, little knowing that she was the last person who would see him alive.

For next morning he awoke between five and six o'clock, got up, and walked towards his dressing table. And it was then, in a moment, that the bright prospect of which he had spoken just four days earlier became, for George Müller, a glorious reality.

21: In every believer

At about seven on the Thursday morning, Müller's attendant knocked at his door with a cup of tea. On entering, she found him lying dead on the floor beside his bed.

The news created a sensation in Bristol. The following Monday was the day of the funeral and the city mourned. It is said that nothing like it has been seen there before or since. Firms closed or gave their employees time off to witness the event. On Bristol cathedral and other churches flags flew at half mast and muffled peals were rung.

After the service at Bethesda Chapel, nearly a hundred carriages including the mayor's state coach joined a procession across the river to the cemetery. The bearers carried the coffin through a crowd of about seven thousand people up the hillside to the spot under a yew tree where Mary and Susannah had been buried.

The earthly body of one of the greatest men of faith in the history of the Christian church was laid to rest. But there was a note of triumph as the huge open-air congregation sang in anticipation of those 'yonder bright regions of joy' where George Müller – raised in a new body – would spend eternity with Christ.

To be sure, he was a great man of faith. But in his life-time Müller used to deny that he had been given a special gift of faith.

'My faith,' he said, 'is the same faith which is found in *every believer*. Try it for yourself and you will see the help of God, if you trust in Him.'

People used to ask him how they might have their faith strengthened.

He would reply:

'First, read the Bible carefully and thoughtfully. Then you will learn more and more about God's character – how kind, loving, merciful, wise and faithful He is. Then when difficulties come, you will be able to rest on God's *ability* and *willingness* to help you.

'Second,' said Müller, 'try to keep your conscience clear. Don't make a habit of doing those things which are displeasing to God. Otherwise when your faith is tested, you will have no confidence in God because of your guilty conscience.

'Third, don't try to avoid situations where your faith might be tested. Naturally we don't like trusting in God alone but it is when we do this that our faith is strengthened.

'Finally, remember that God will not test you more than you are able to bear. Be patient, and He will prove to you how willing He is to help and deliver, the moment it is good for you.'

God has not changed since Müller's day. The work of the homes has. In this century, the directors have adapted to two main changes: new ideas about how children should be cared for, and changing social conditions which have meant that children need care for different reasons.

The great buildings on Ashley Down have been sold and are now the headquarters of Brunel Technical College. The children are looked after by house parents in more luxurious small family group homes, and attend local schools.

But even this type of residential care where the children 'live in' is coming to an end. Children are now usually fostered with individual families. And advances in medicine mean that there are in any case very few children who have been made orphans in the way that George Müller knew. But there are different problems: family units are less secure or may not exist at all. So the Müller Homes are opening Day Care and Family Care Centres to try to help those children who, still today, are in desperate need.

'Glandore', the first Müller's Day Care Centre in Weston-Super-Mare, reaches out to the community, not only to the children but also to their parents. There is a waiting list of children of pre-school age whose mothers are for various reasons unable themselves to look after them during the day.

The first Family Care Centres are soon to be opened: one in Weston-Super-Mare and another in Bristol. Each of these will care for up to five families in lots of ways including holding groups which will discuss the Christian gospel.

There are far more old people in England than ever before. The directors are hoping to establish 'The Müller Homes for the Elderly'. This will be expensive, but if it is God's will, He will supply the funds just as He did in George Müller's day.

Gifts are still sent regularly to missionaries in many parts of the world – nearly £40,000 in 1983. Some of this money comes from the profit earned by two busy bookshops run by Müller's in Bristol and Bath. These two shops – called Evangelical Christian Literature – also supply over one hundred church bookstalls. So the tradition established when Müller opened his Bible warehouse in 1849 is continued – but, as you will discover if you visit the bookshops, in a style which is right for the late twentieth century. As the homes adapt, the importance attached to prayer and faith remains. Mr Rose and Mr Cowan, who now have the responsibility which George Müller once bore, look to God to provide for every daily need and to guide them in their plans for future ventures.

Mr Rose wrote recently:

'As God was in our yesterday, He is in our today and will be in our tomorrow.' Depending on this, the homes launch out in faith for the future.